INCLUDES CD

Orchestrated arrangements with you as the soloist!

Andrew Lloyd Webber™ Hits

ISBN 978-1-4234-5894-4

Hal•Leonard® Corporation

7777 W. Bluemound Rd. P.O. Box 13819 Milwaukee, WI 53213

Visit Hal Leonard Online at
www.halleonard.com

CLOSE EVERY DOOR TO ME

from JOSEPH AND THE AMAZING TECHNICOLOR® DREAMCOAT

Music by ANDREW LLOYD WEBBER
Lyrics by TIM RICE

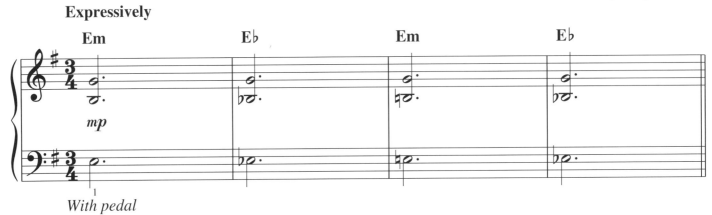

Close ev - 'ry door to me, hide all the world from me.

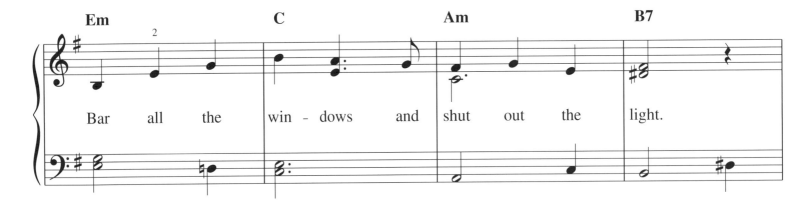

Bar all the win - dows and shut out the light.

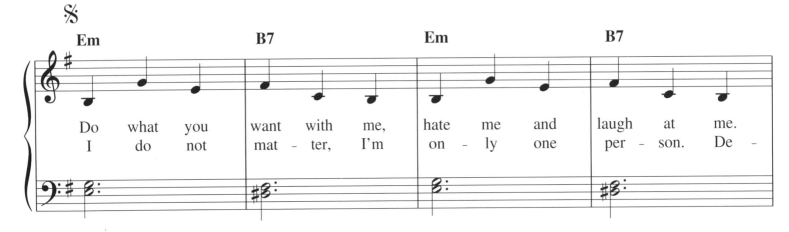

Do what you want with me, hate me and laugh at me.
I do not mat - ter, I'm on - ly one per - son. De -

Dark - en my day - time and tor - ture my night.
stroy me com - plete - ly and throw me a - way. If my

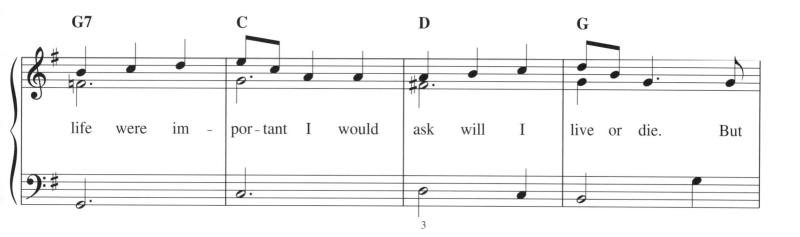

life were im - por - tant I would ask will I live or die. But

To Coda ⊕

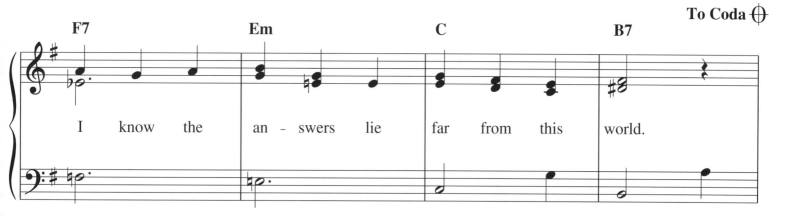

I know the an - swers lie far from this world.

Close ev - 'ry door to me, keep those I love from me.

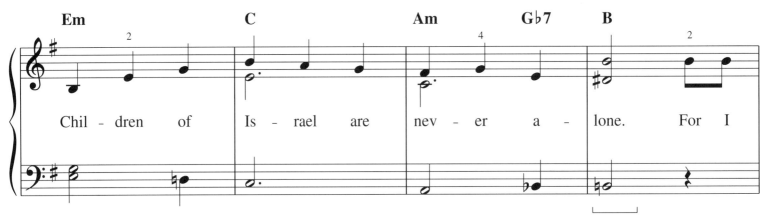

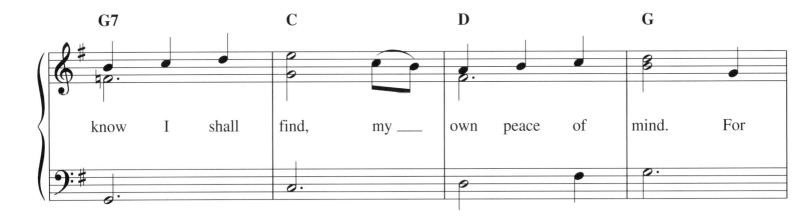

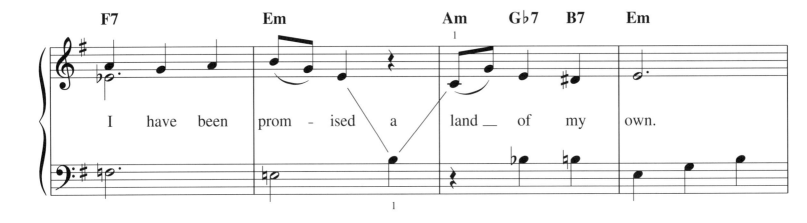

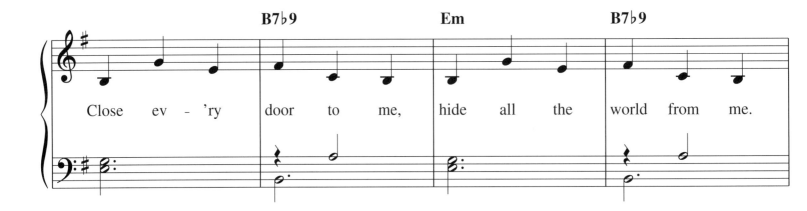

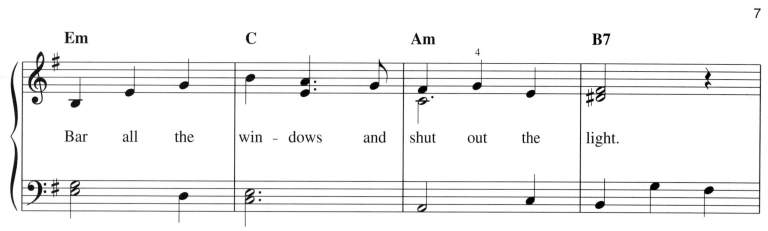

Bar all the win - dows and shut out the light.

La la la la la la la la la la la la la la la la la la

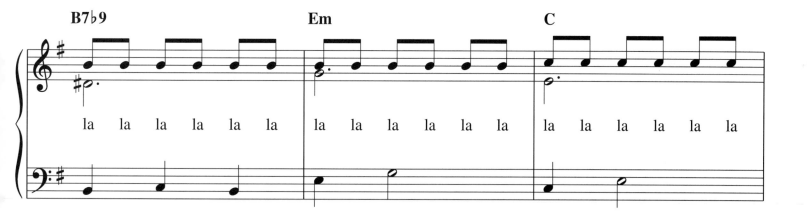

la la la la la la la la la la la la la la la la la la

la la la la la la la.

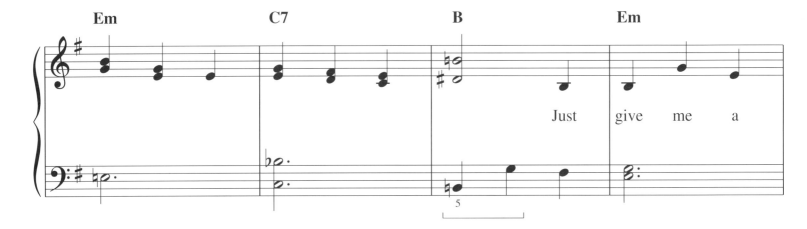

Just give me a

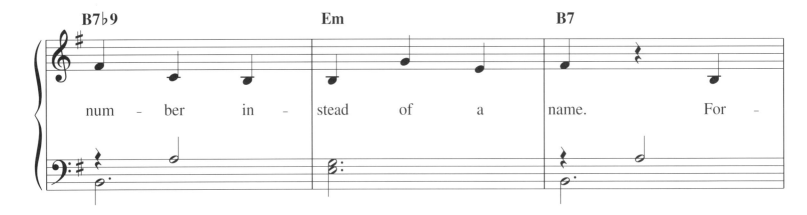

num – ber in – stead of a name. For –

D.S. al Coda

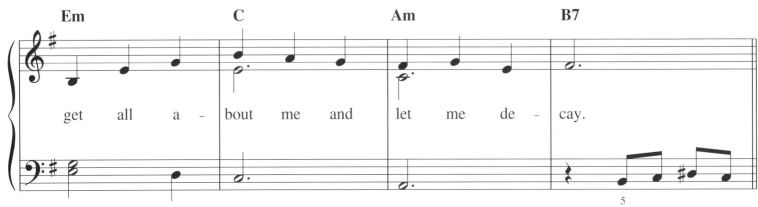

get all a – bout me and let me de – cay.

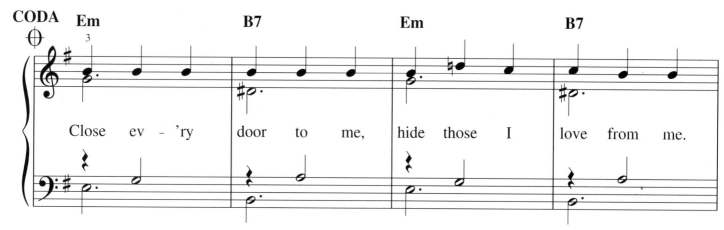

Close ev – 'ry door to me, hide those I love from me.

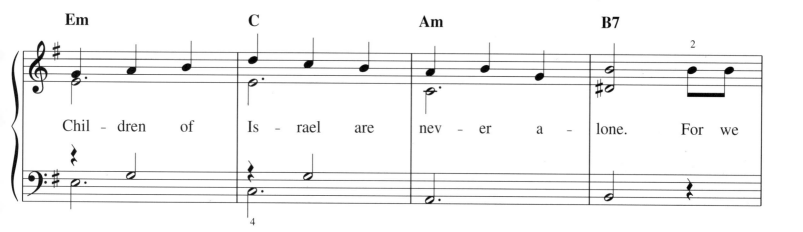

Chil – dren of Is – rael are nev – er a – lone. For we

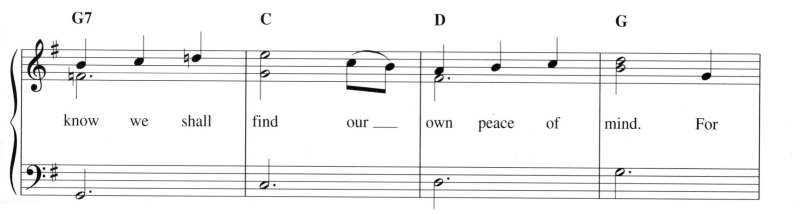

know we shall find our ___ own peace of mind. For

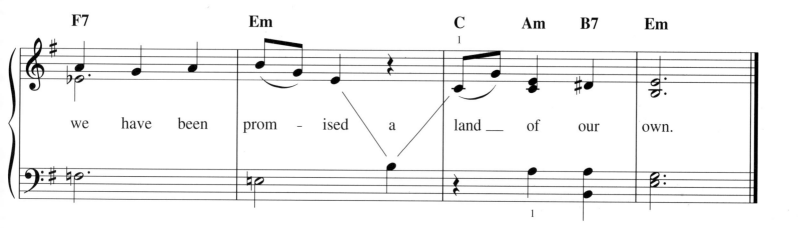

we have been prom – ised a land ___ of our own.

DON'T CRY FOR ME ARGENTINA

from EVITA

Words by TIM RICE
Music by ANDREW LLOYD WEBBER

Moderate Tango tempo

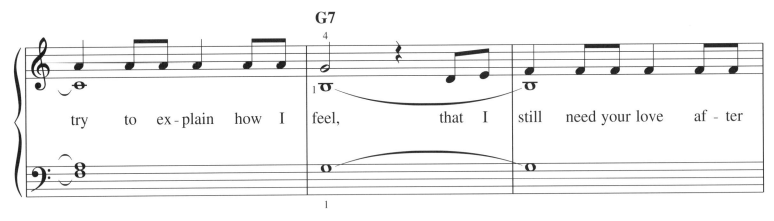

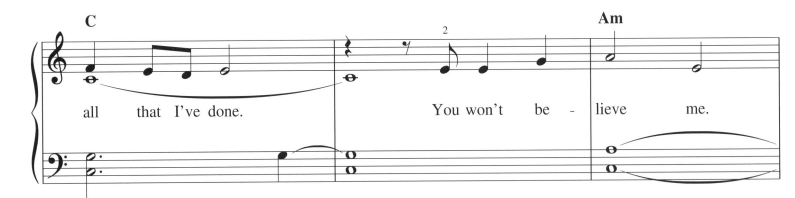

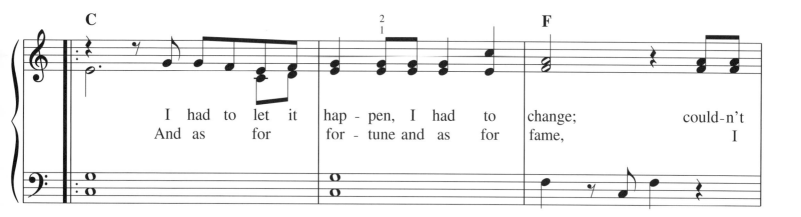

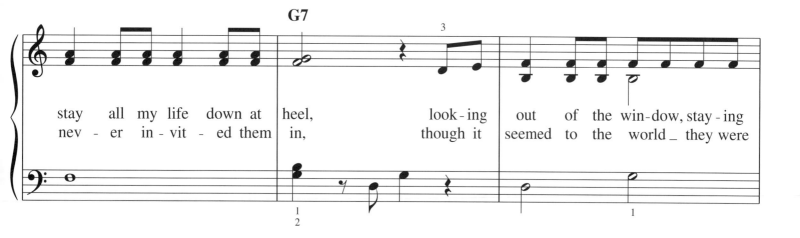

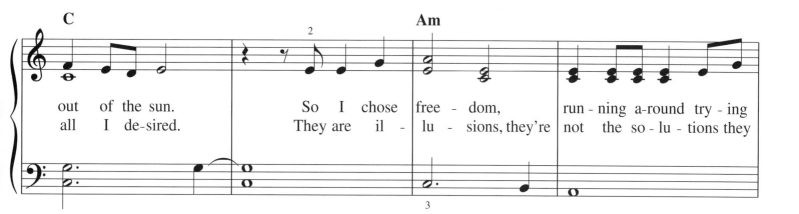

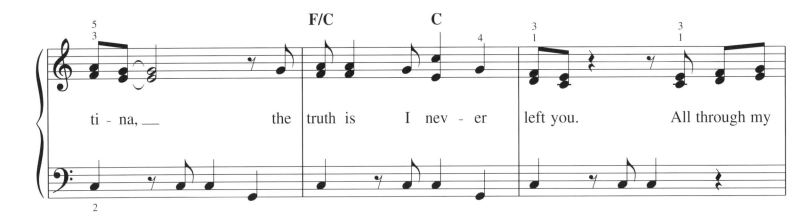

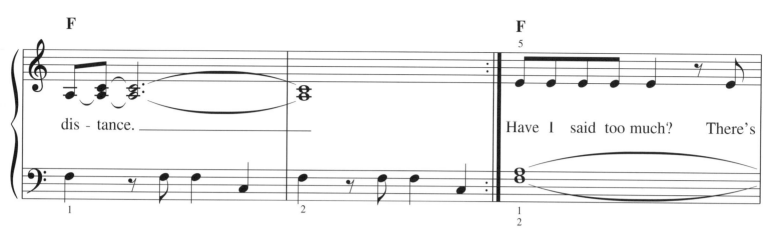

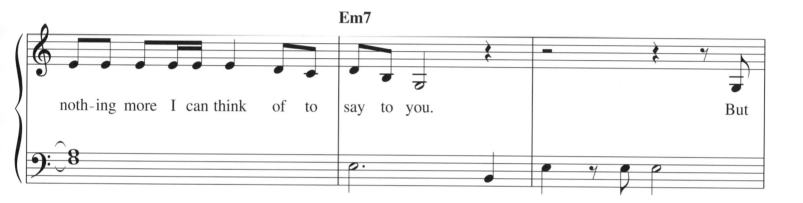

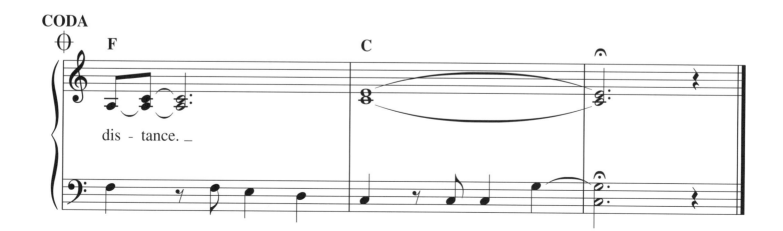

I DON'T KNOW HOW TO LOVE HIM

from JESUS CHRIST SUPERSTAR

Words by TIM RICE
Music by ANDREW LLOYD WEBBER

Slowly and tenderly

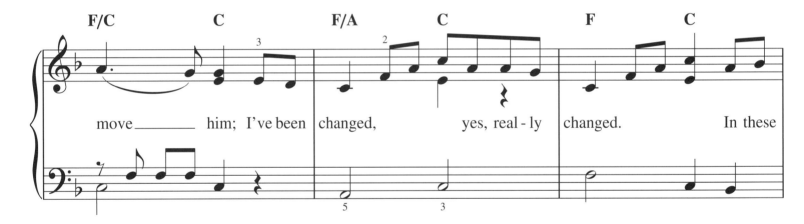

else. I don't know how to take_____ this,

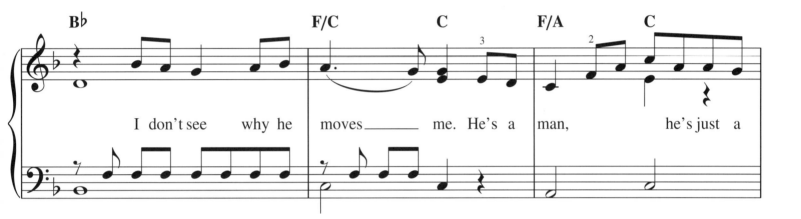

I don't see why he moves_____ me. He's a man, he's just a

man, and I've had so man - y men be - fore in

ver - y man - y ways._____ He's just one more.

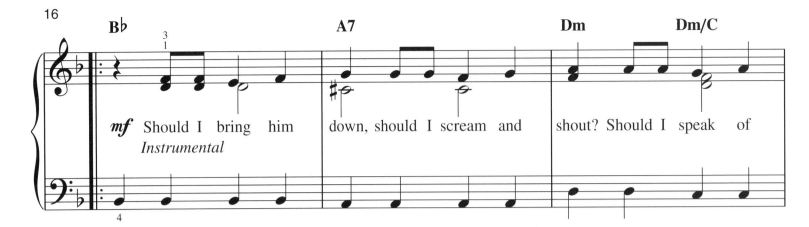

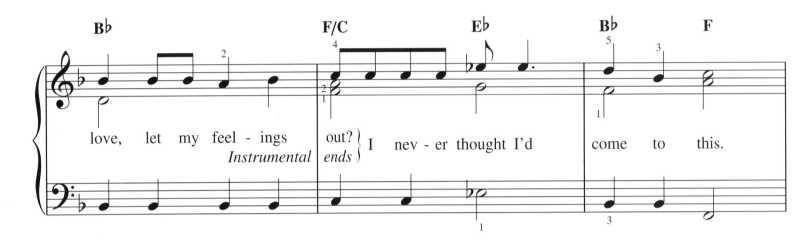

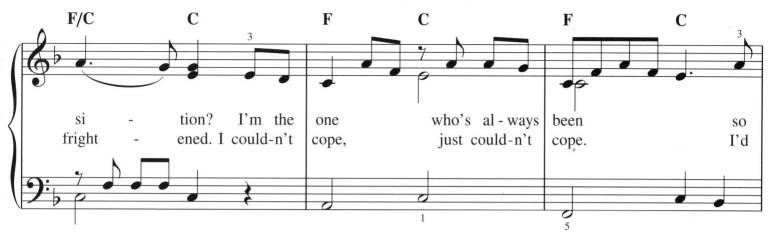

si - tion? I'm the one who's al - ways been so
fright - ened. I could-n't cope, just could-n't cope. I'd

calm, so cool, no lov-er's fool, run - ning ev - 'ry____
turn my head, I'd back a - way, I would-n't want to____

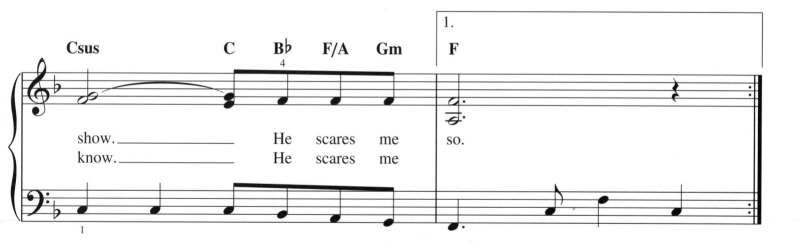

show._____ He scares me so.
know._____ He scares me

1.

2.

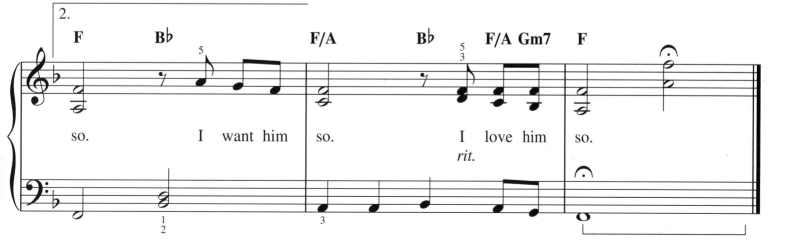

so. I want him so. I love him so.
rit.

LOVE CHANGES EVERYTHING

from ASPECTS OF LOVE

Music by ANDREW LLOYD WEBBER
Lyrics by DON BLACK and CHARLES HART

Moderately

Love,   love chang- es   ev - ery-thing: hands and   fac - es,   earth and

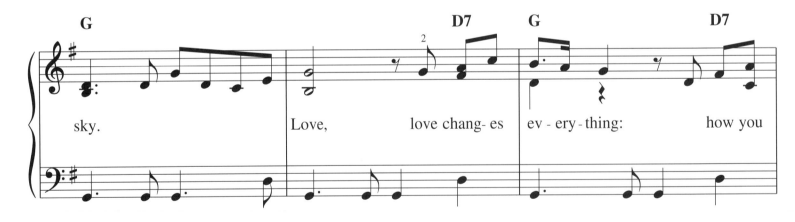

sky.   Love,   love chang- es   ev - ery-thing: how you

live and   how you   die.   Love   can make the

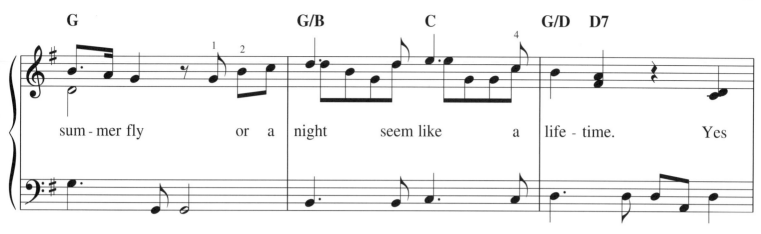

sum - mer fly   or   a   night   seem like   a   life - time.   Yes

love,   love chang-es   ev - ery-thing: now I   trem - ble   at your

name.   Noth-ing   in   the world will   ev - er   be   the

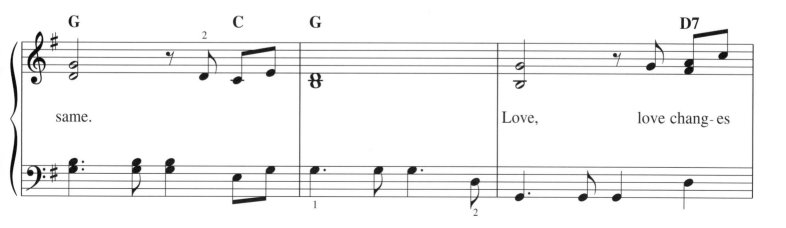

same.   Love,   love chang- es

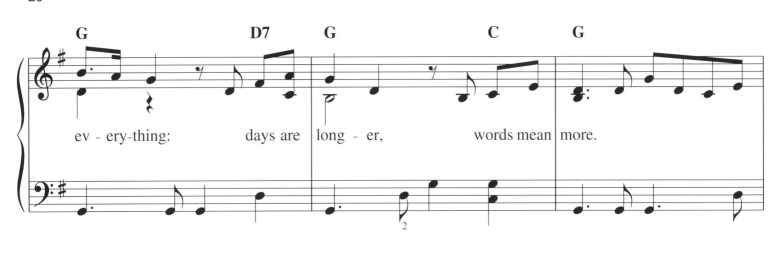

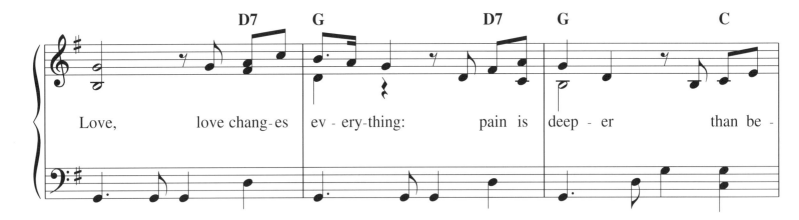

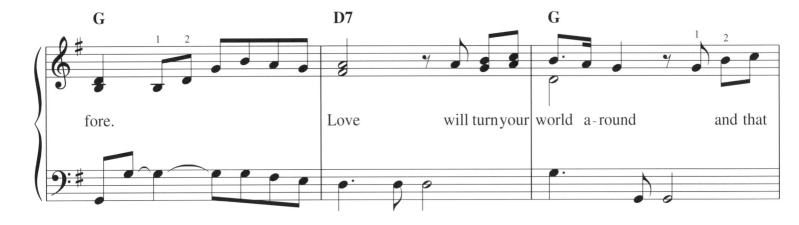

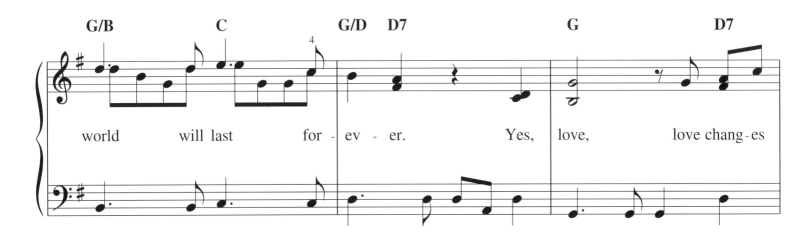

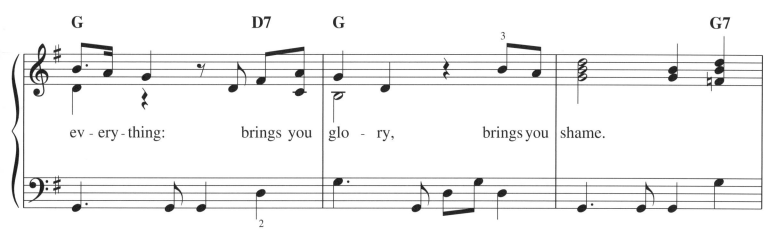

ev - ery - thing: brings you glo - ry,   brings you shame.

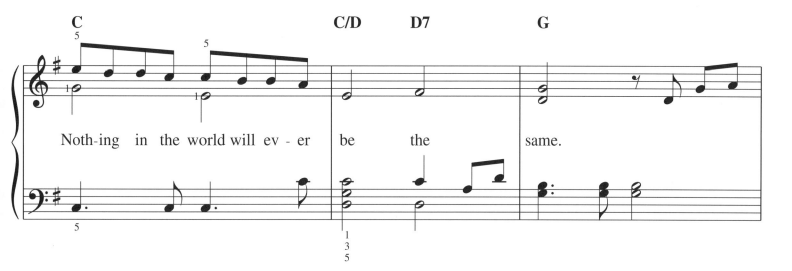

Noth-ing in the world will ev - er   be   the   same.

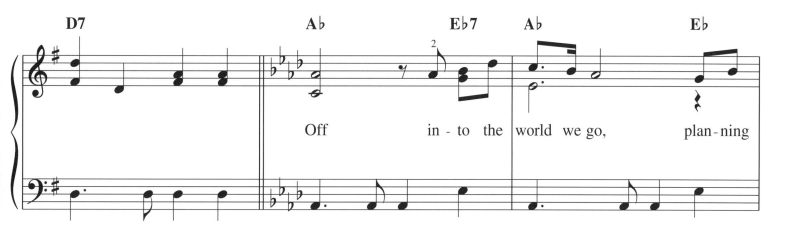

Off   in - to the world we go,   plan - ning

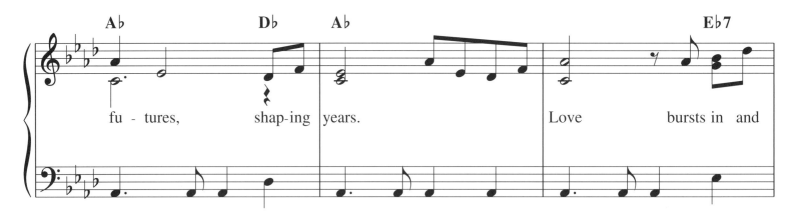

fu - tures, shap-ing years. Love bursts in and

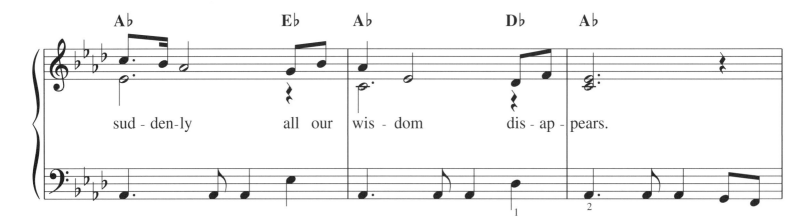

sud - den-ly all our wis - dom dis - ap - pears.

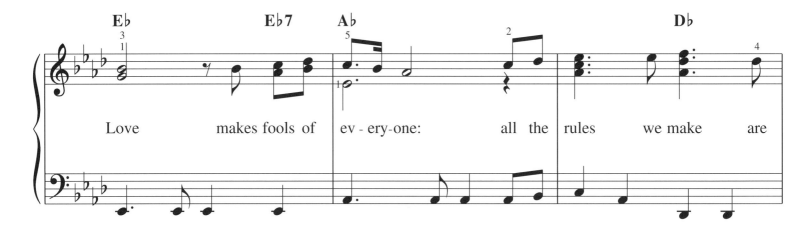

Love makes fools of ev - ery-one: all the rules we make are

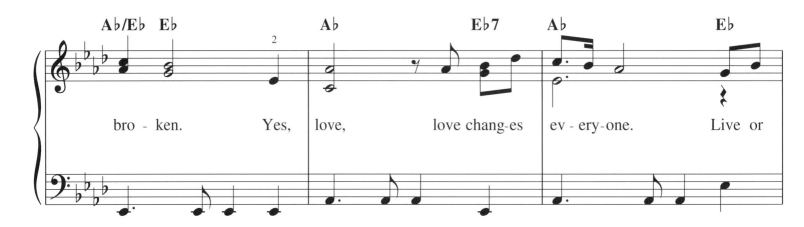

bro - ken. Yes, love, love chang-es ev - ery-one. Live or

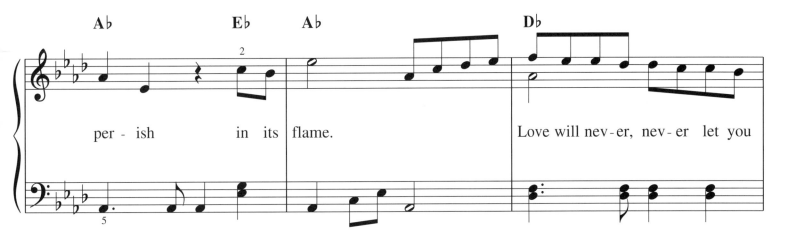

per - ish   in its flame.   Love will nev - er, nev - er let you

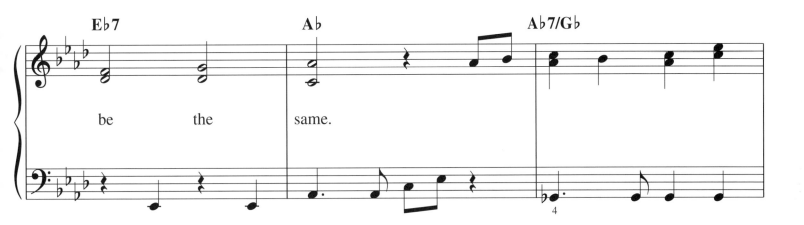

be   the   same.

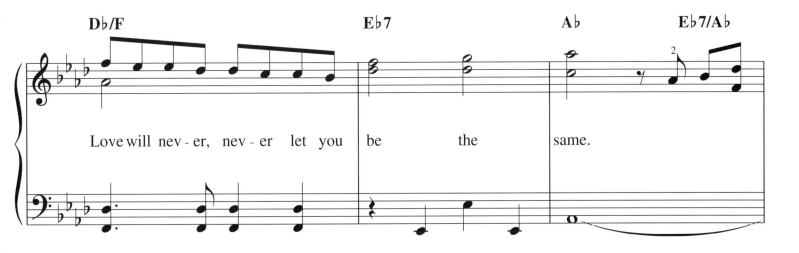

Love will nev - er, nev - er let you   be   the   same.

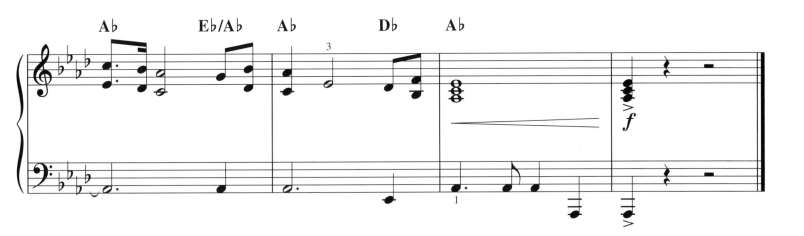

THE MUSIC OF THE NIGHT

from THE PHANTOM OF THE OPERA

Music by ANDREW LLOYD WEBBER
Lyrics by CHARLES HART
Additional Lyrics by RICHARD STILGOE

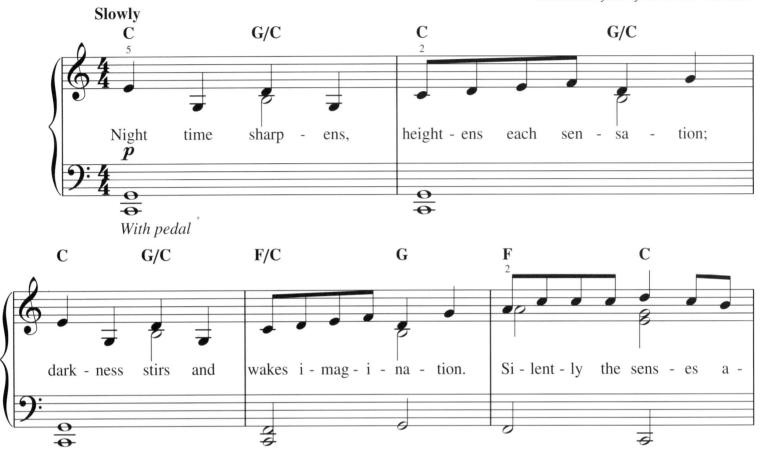

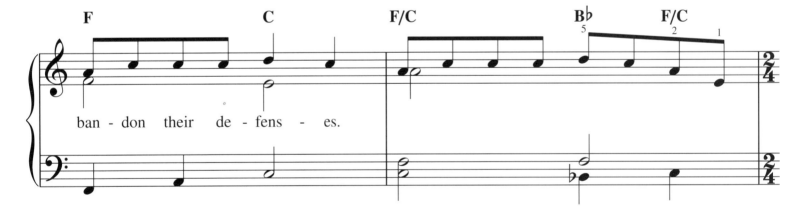

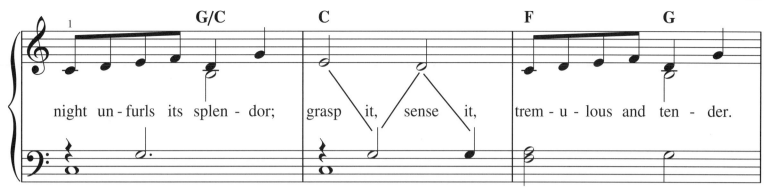

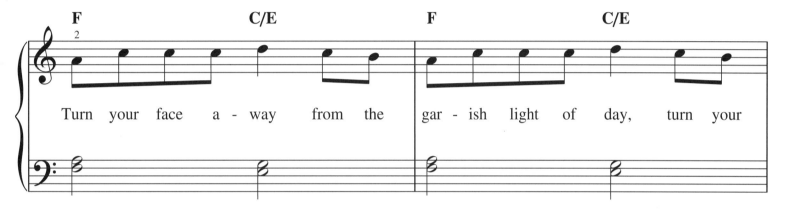

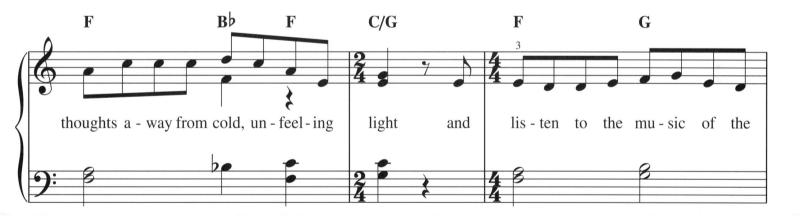

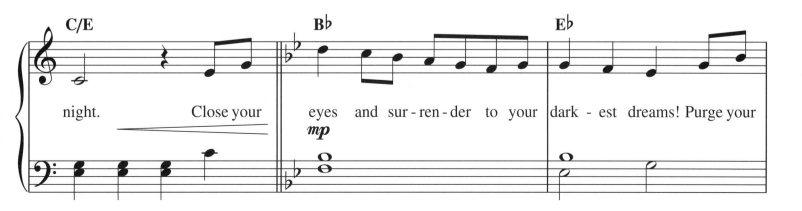

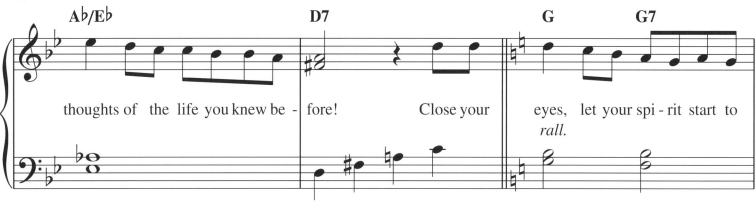

thoughts of the life you knew be - fore! Close your eyes, let your spi - rit start to *rall.*

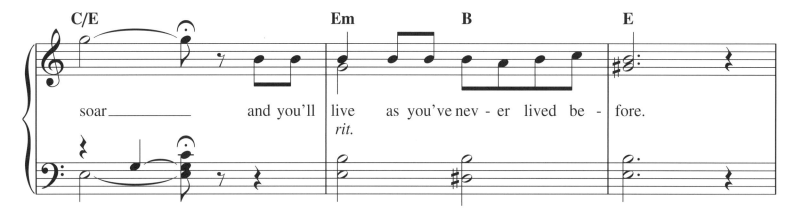

soar _____ and you'll live as you've nev - er lived be - fore. *rit.*

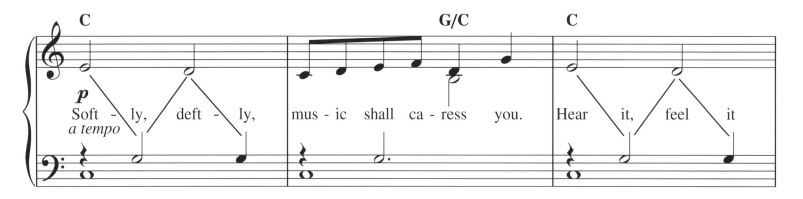

p Soft - ly, deft - ly, mus - ic shall ca - ress you. Hear it, feel it *a tempo*

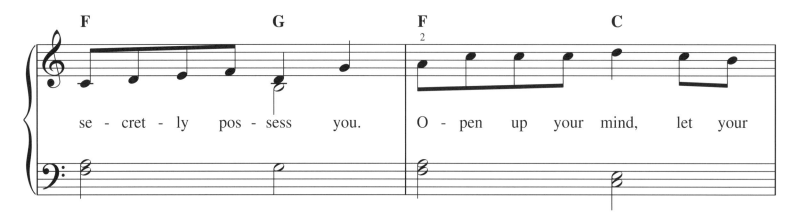

se - cret - ly pos - sess you. O - pen up your mind, let your

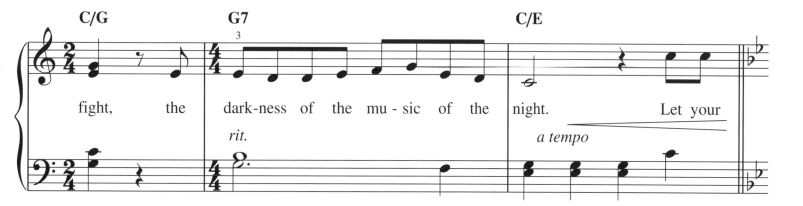

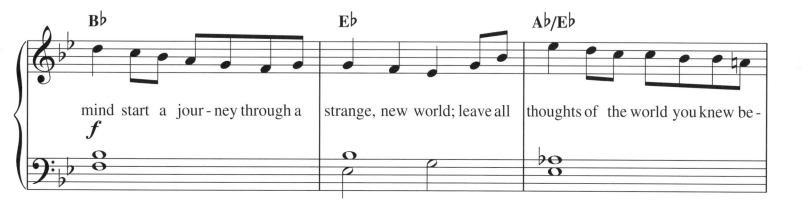

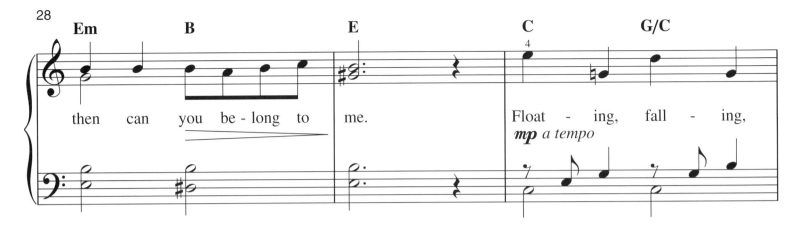

then can you be-long to me. Floating, falling,
mp a tempo

sweet in-tox-i-ca - tion. Touch me, trust me, sa - vor each sen - sa - tion.

Let the dream be - gin, let your dark - er side give in to the

pow - er of the mu - sic that I write, the pow - er of the mu - sic of the
rit.

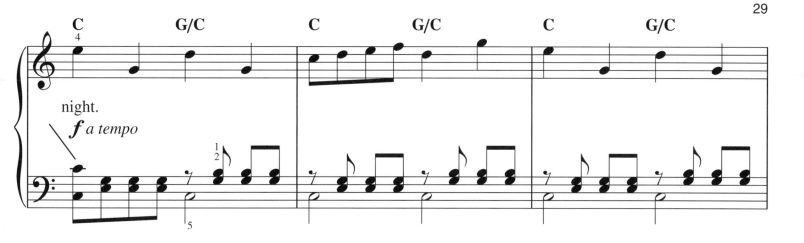

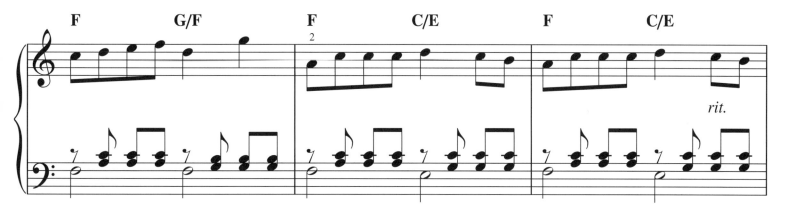

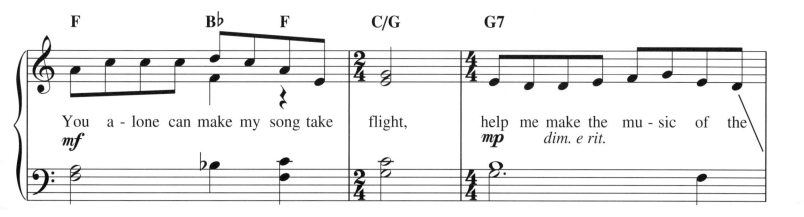

You a - lone can make my song take flight, help me make the mu - sic of the

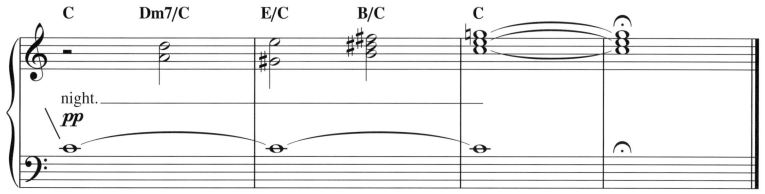

night.

NO MATTER WHAT
from WHISTLE DOWN THE WIND

Music by ANDREW LLOYD WEBBER
Lyrics by JIM STEINMAN

No mat - ter what they
If on - ly tears they were

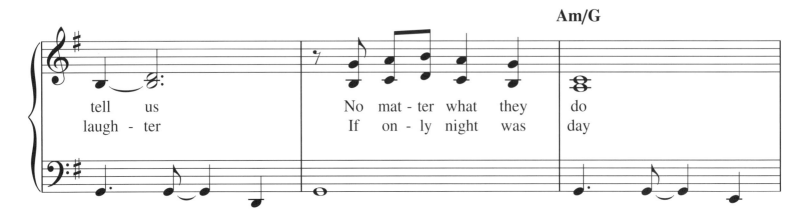

tell us
laugh - ter

No mat - ter what they
If on - ly night was

do
day

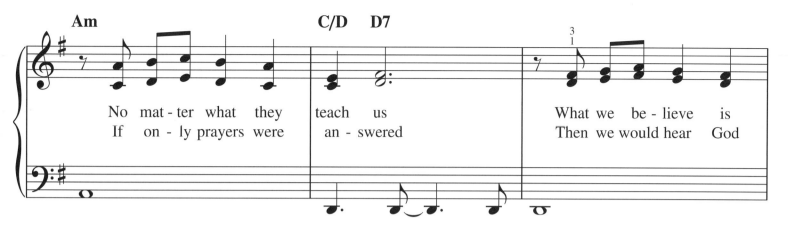

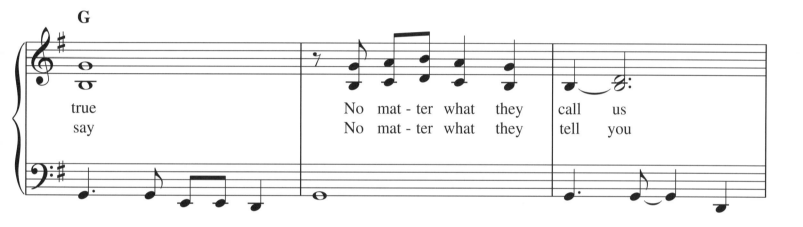

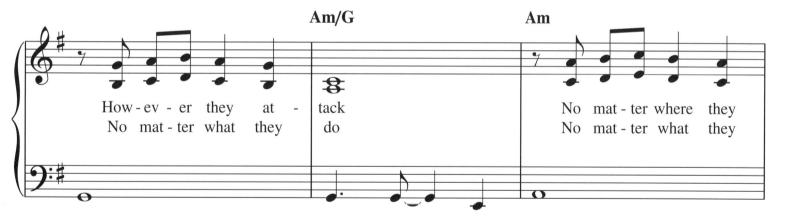

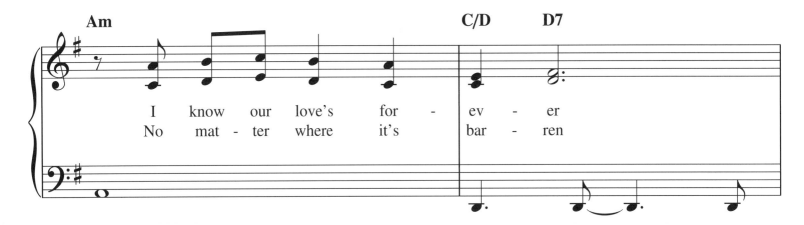

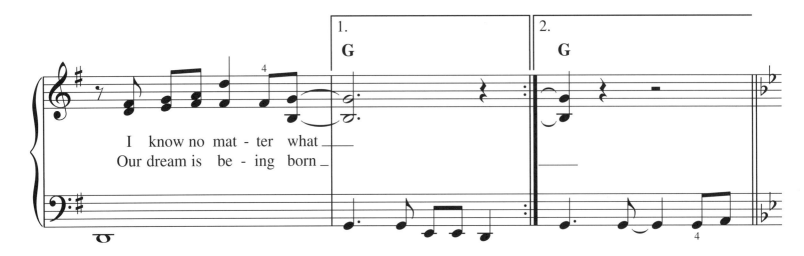

No mat - ter who they fol - low

No mat - ter where they

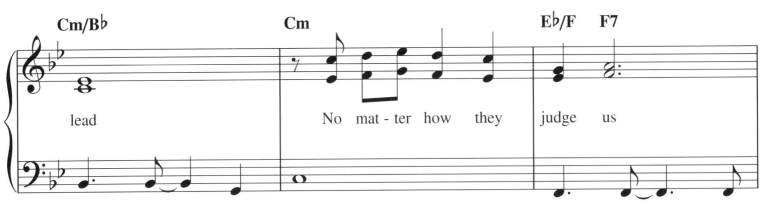

lead   No mat - ter how they   judge us

I'll be ev - 'ry one you need. _____ No

mat - ter if _____ the sun ____ don't shine ____
can't de - ny _____ what I ____ be - lieve, ___

or if the _____ skies are blue ____
I can't be _____ what I'm not.

1.

Cm

Eb/F　**F7**

No mat - ter what the　end - ing　my life be - gan with

Bb

you　I

2.
Slowly
Cm

F7

I know this love's　for - ev - er　that's all that

Cm　　**F7**

Tempo I
Bb

mat - ters now no mat - ter　what
rit.

mp

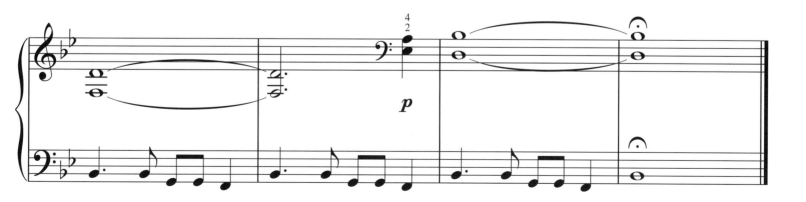

p

PIE JESU

from REQUIEM

By ANDREW LLOYD WEBBER

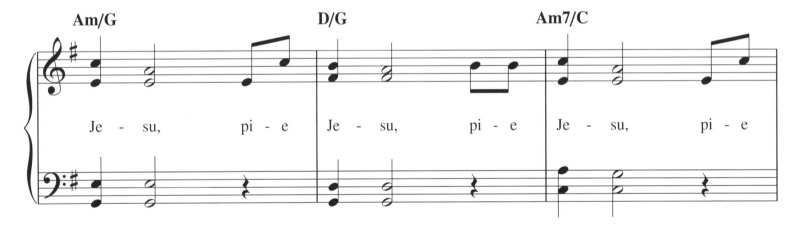

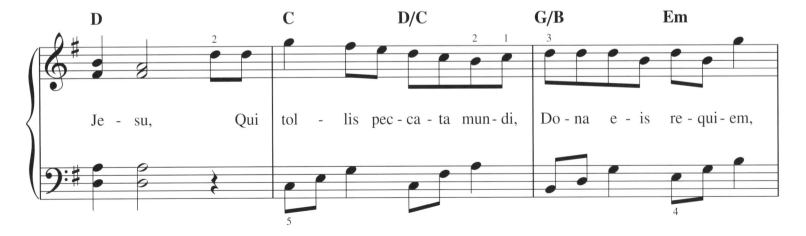

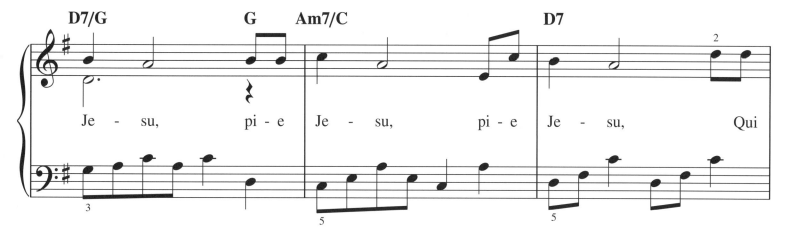

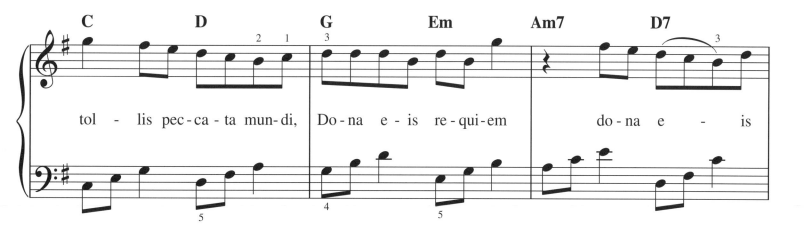

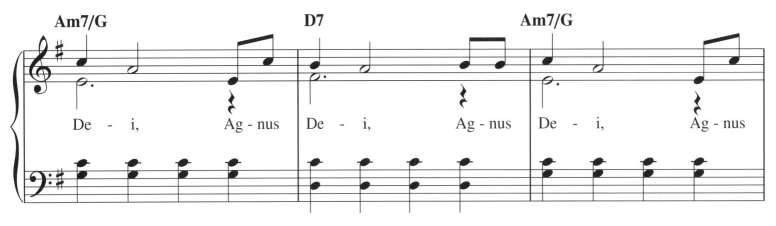

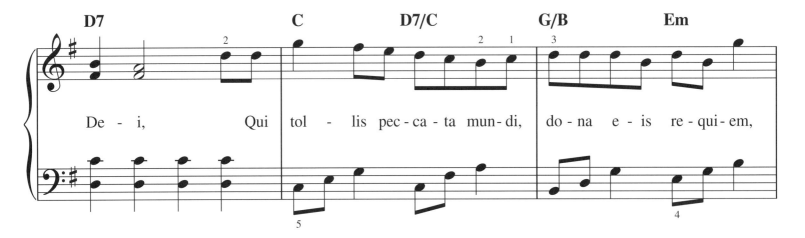

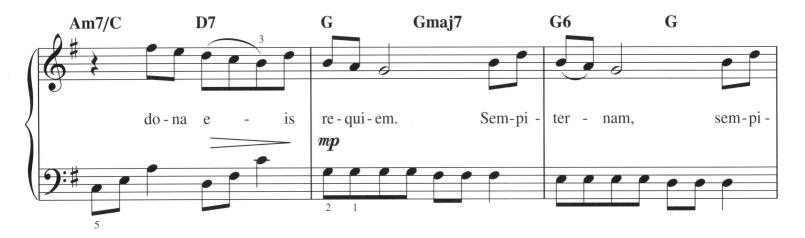

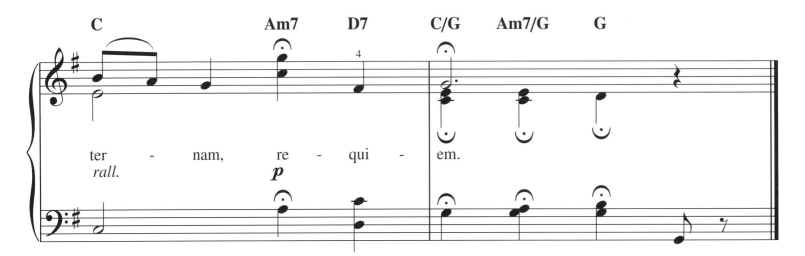

TELL ME ON A SUNDAY

from SONG & DANCE

Music by ANDREW LLOYD WEBBER
Lyrics by DON BLACK

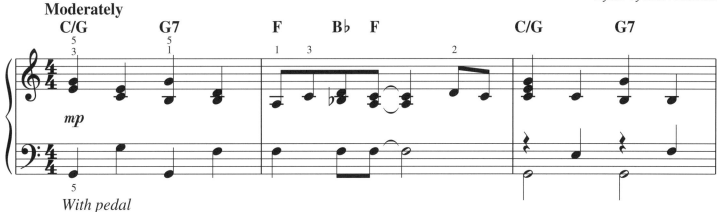

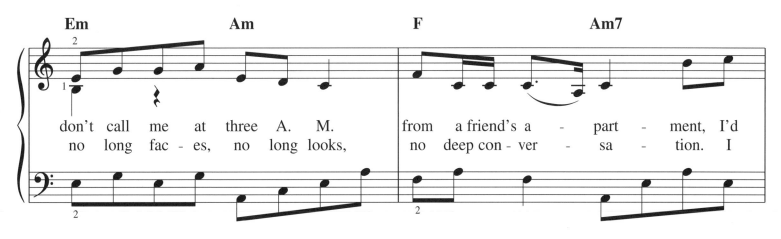

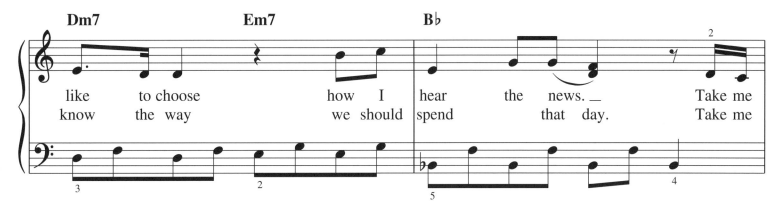

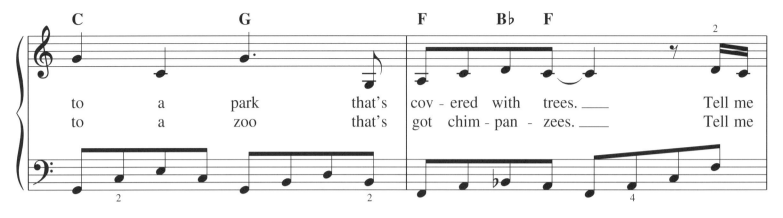

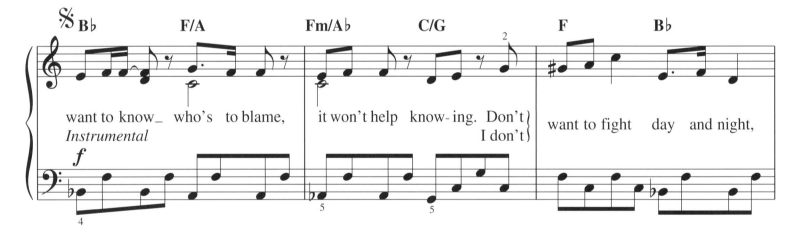

Em   Am   F   Am7

Don't get drunk and slam the door. __ That's no way to end this. I

Dm7   Em7   B♭   C   G

know how I want you to say good-bye. Find a cir - cus ring with a

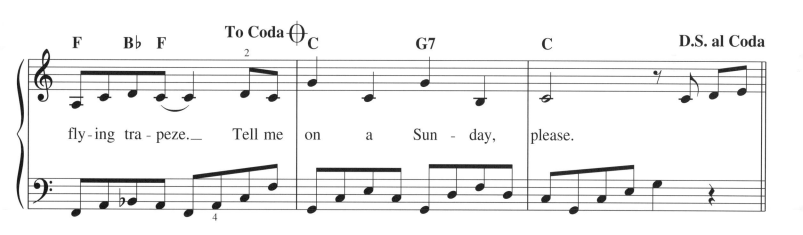

F   B♭   F   **To Coda**   C   G7   C   **D.S. al Coda**

fly-ing tra - peze.__ Tell me on a Sun - day, please.

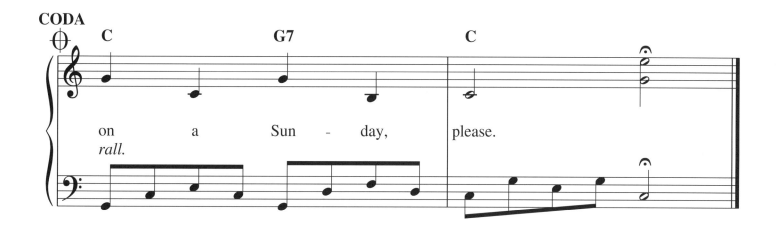

CODA

C   G7   C

on a Sun - day, please.

rall.

WITH ONE LOOK

from SUNSET BOULEVARD

Music by ANDREW LLOYD WEBBER
Lyrics by DON BLACK and CHRISTOPHER HAMPTON,
with contributions by AMY POWERS

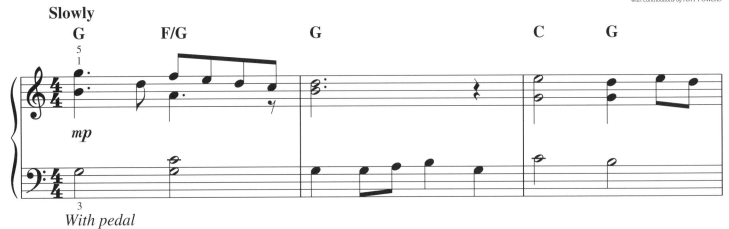

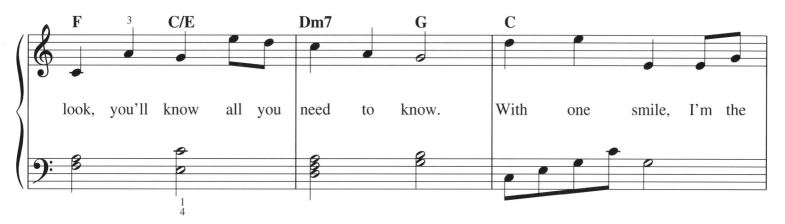

look, you'll know all you need to know. With one smile, I'm the

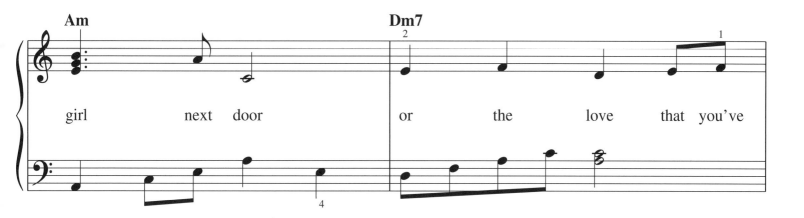

girl next door or the love that you've

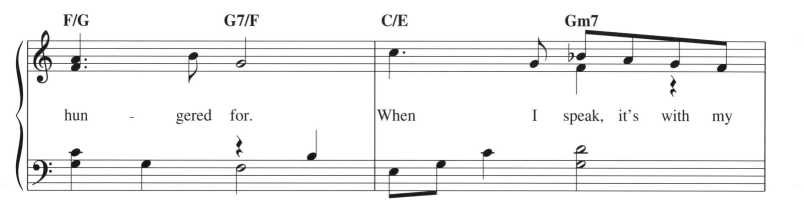

hun - gered for. When I speak, it's with my

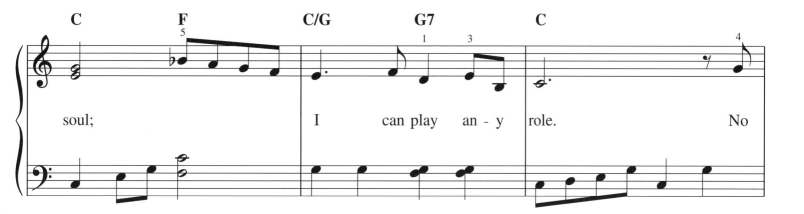

soul; I can play an - y role. No

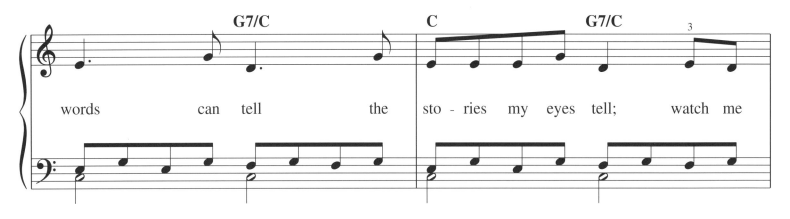

words   can tell   the   sto - ries   my   eyes tell;   watch me

when   I   frown,   you   can't   write   that   down.   You

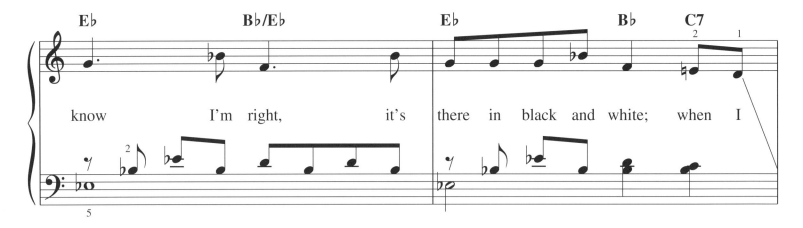

know   I'm   right,   it's   there   in   black   and   white;   when   I

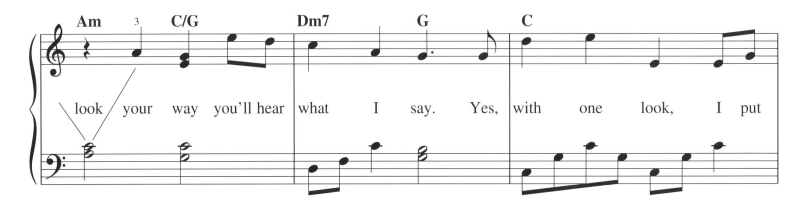

look / your   way   you'll hear   what   I   say.   Yes,   with   one   look,   I   put

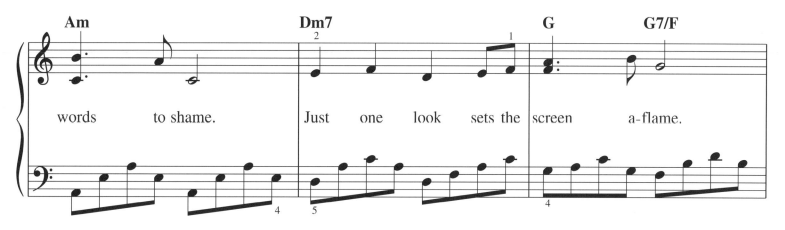

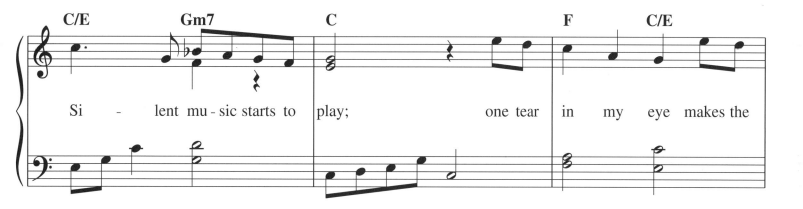

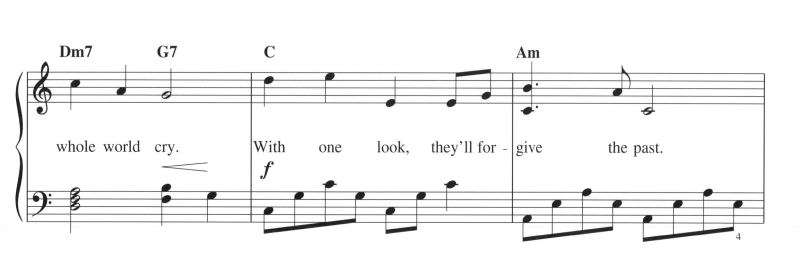

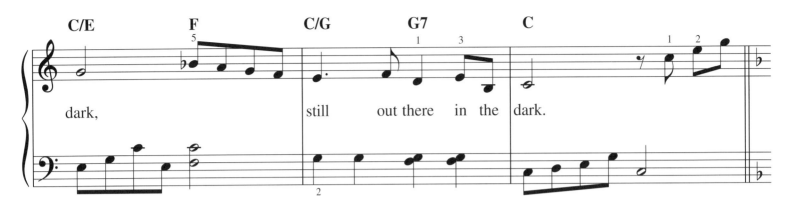

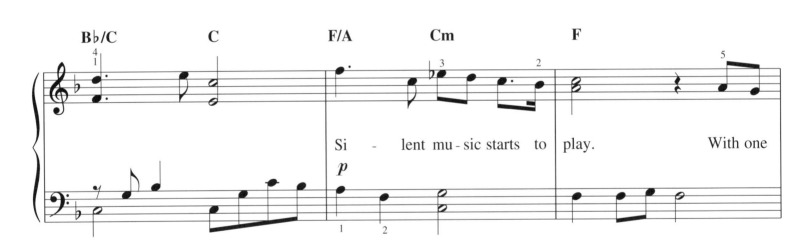

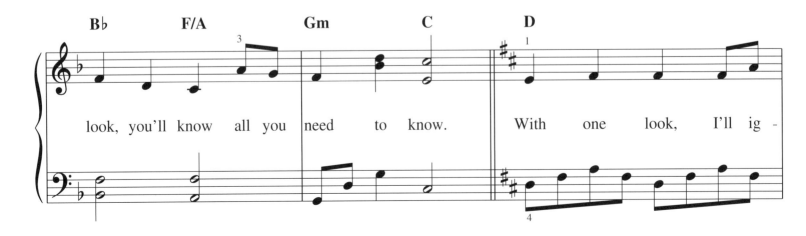

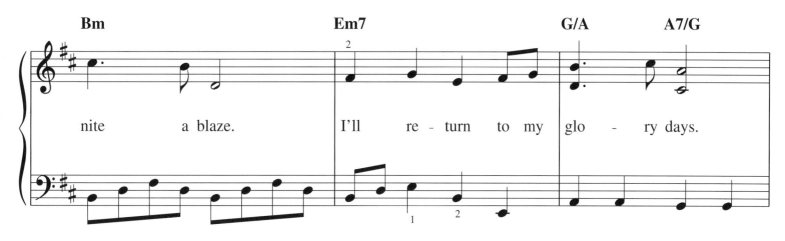

Bm   **Em7**   **G/A**   **A7/G**

nite   a blaze.   I'll re - turn to my glo - ry days.

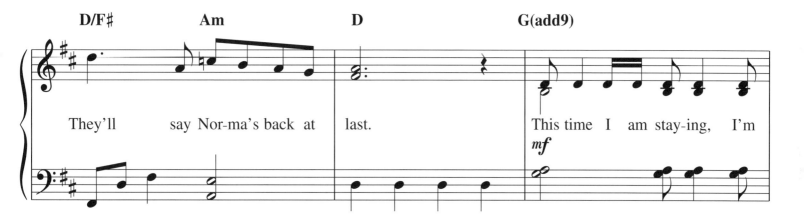

D/F♯   **Am**   **D**   **G(add9)**

They'll   say Nor-ma's back at   last.   This time I am stay-ing, I'm

mf

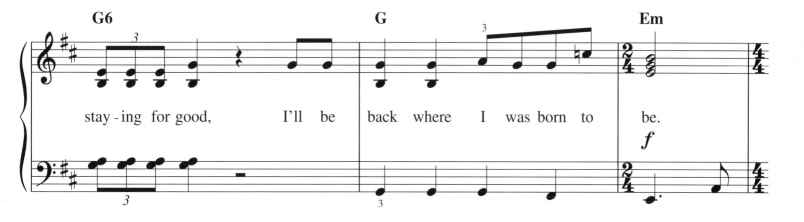

G6   **G**   **Em**

stay - ing for good,   I'll be   back where I was born to   be.

f

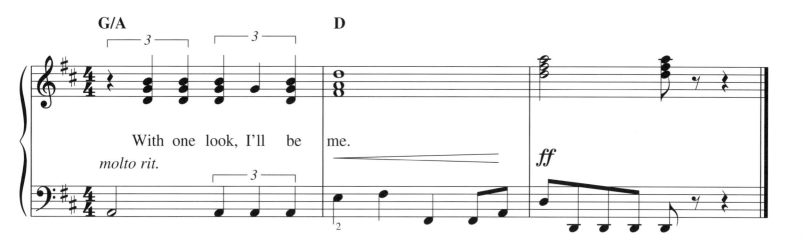

G/A   **D**

With one look, I'll be   me.

molto rit.

ff

WISHING YOU WERE SOMEHOW HERE AGAIN

from THE PHANTOM OF THE OPERA

Music by ANDREW LLOYD WEBBER
Lyrics by CHARLES HART
Additional Lyrics by RICHARD STILGOE

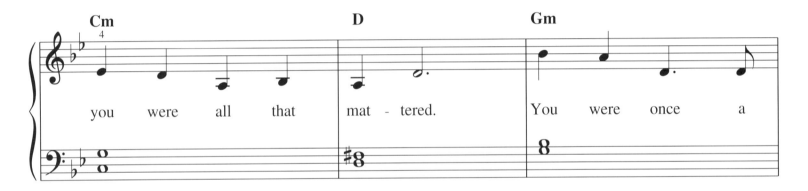

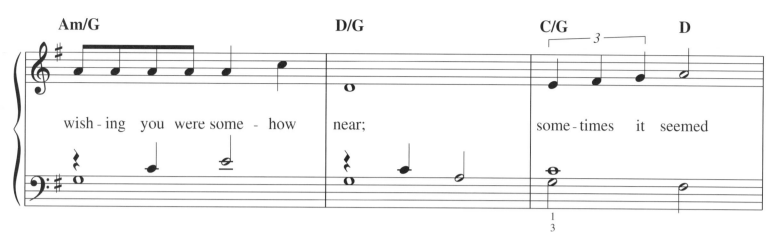

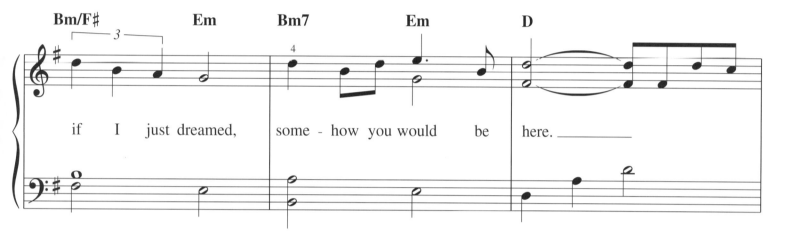

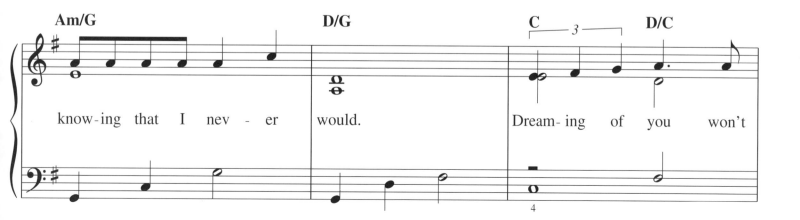

help me to do all that you dreamed I could.

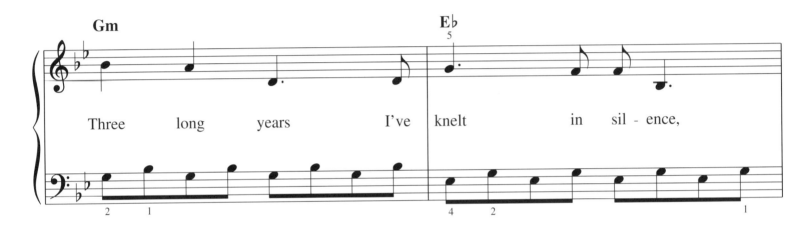

Three long years I've knelt in sil - ence,

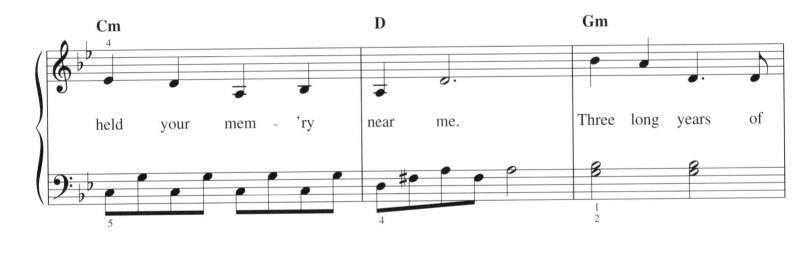

held your mem - 'ry near me. Three long years of

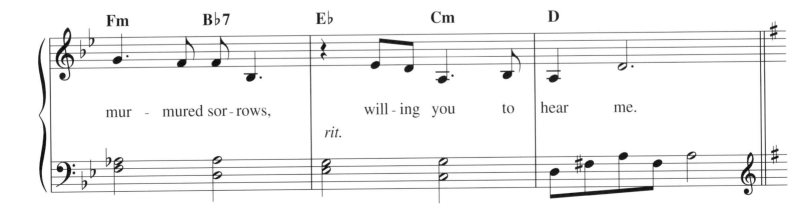

mur - mured sor - rows, will - ing you to hear me.

rit.

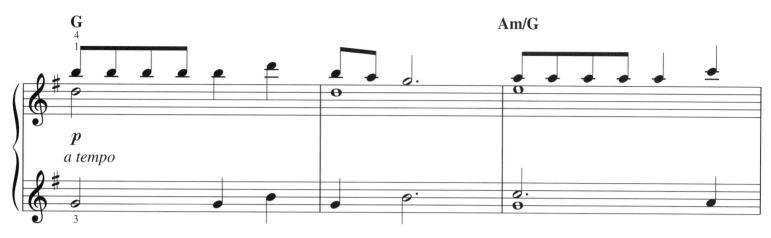

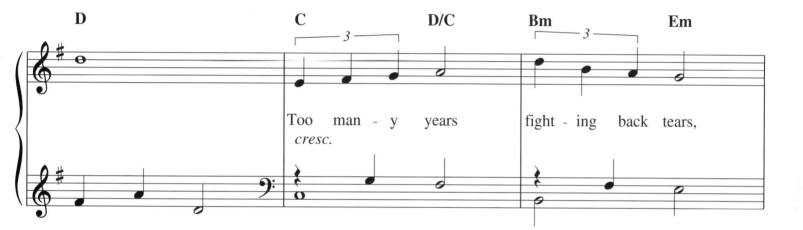

Too man - y years   fight - ing back tears,

cresc.

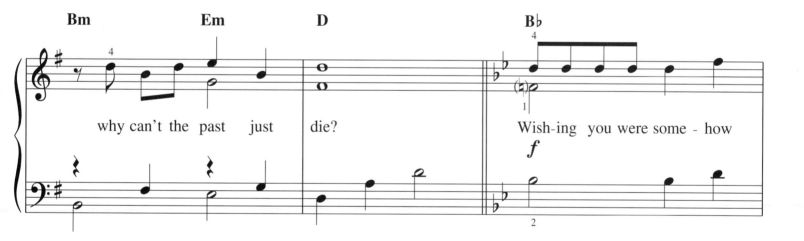

why can't the past just   die?

Wish-ing you were some - how

f

here a - gain,

know - ing we must say   good - bye.

rit.

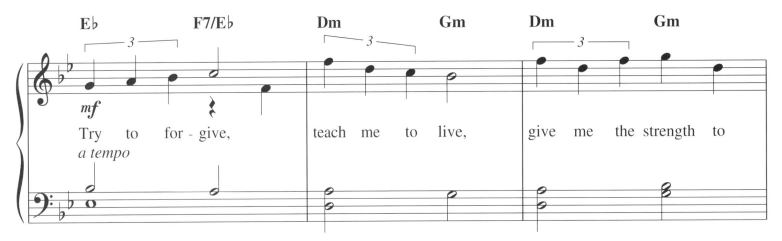

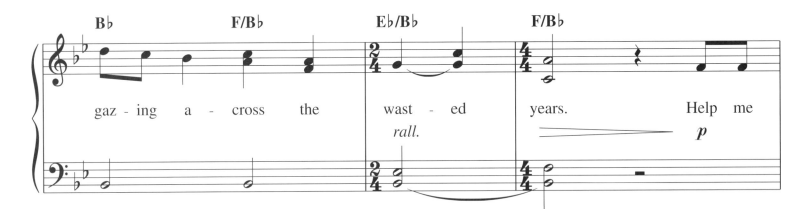

EASY PIANO CD PLAY-ALONGS

Orchestrated arrangements with you as the soloist!

This series lets you play along with great accompaniments to songs you know and love! Each book comes with a CD of complete professional performances and includes matching custom arrangements in Easy Piano format. With these books you can: Listen to complete professional performances of each of the songs; Play the Easy Piano arrangements along with the performances; Sing along with the recordings; Play the Easy Piano arrangements as solos, without the CD.

GREAT JAZZ STANDARDS – VOLUME 1
Bewitched • Don't Get Around Much Anymore • How Deep Is the Ocean • It Might As Well Be Spring • My Funny Valentine • Satin Doll • Stardust • and more.
00310916 Easy Piano $14.95

FAVORITE CLASSICAL THEMES – VOLUME 2
Bach: Air on the G String • Beethoven: Symphony No. 5, Excerpt • Gounod: Ave Maria • Grieg: Morning • Handel: Hallelujah Chorus • Pachelbel: Canon • Tchaikovsky: Waltz of the Flowers • and more.
00310921 Easy Piano $14.95

BROADWAY FAVORITES – VOLUME 3
All I Ask of You • Beauty and the Beast • Bring Him Home • Cabaret • Close Every Door • I've Never Been in Love Before • If I Loved You • Memory • My Favorite Things • Some Enchanted Evening.
00310915 Easy Piano $14.95

ADULT CONTEMPORARY HITS – VOLUME 4
Amazed • Angel • Breathe • I Don't Want to Wait • I Hope You Dance • I Will Remember You • I'll Be • It's Your Love • The Power of Love • You'll Be in My Heart.
00310919 Easy Piano $14.95

HIT POP/ROCK BALLADS – VOLUME 5
Don't Let the Sun Go Down on Me • From a Distance • I Can't Make You Love Me • I'll Be There • Imagine • In My Room • Rainy Days and Mondays • Total Eclipse of the Heart • and more.
00310917 Easy Piano $14.95

LOVE SONG FAVORITES – VOLUME 6
Fields of Gold • I Honestly Love You • If • Lady in Red • More Than Words • Save the Best for Last • Three Times a Lady • Up Where We Belong • We've Only Just Begun • You Are So Beautiful.
00310918 Easy Piano $14.95

O HOLY NIGHT – VOLUME 7
Angels We Have Heard on High • God Rest Ye Merry, Gentlemen • It Came upon the Midnight Clear • O Holy Silent Night • What Child Is This? • and more.
00310920 Easy Piano $14.95

A CHRISTIAN WEDDING – VOLUME 8
Cherish the Treasure • Commitment Song • How Beautiful • I Will Be Here • In This Very Room • The Lord's Prayer • Love Will Be Our Home • Parent's Prayer • This Is the Day • The Wedding.
00311104 Easy Piano $14.95

COUNTRY BALLADS – VOLUME 9
Always on My Mind • Could I Have This Dance • Crazy • Crying • Forever and Ever, Amen • He Stopped Loving Her Today • I Can Love You Like That • The Keeper of the Stars • Release Me • When You Say Nothing at All.
00311105 Easy Piano $14.95

MOVIE GREATS – VOLUME 10
And All That Jazz • Chariots of Fire • Come What May • Forrest Gump • I Finally Found Someone • Iris • Mission: Impossible Theme • Tears in Heaven • There You'll Be • A Wink and a Smile.
00311106 Easy Piano $14.95

DISNEY BLOCKBUSTERS – VOLUME 11
Be Our Guest • Can You Feel the Love Tonight • Go the Distance • Look Through My Eyes • Reflection • Two Worlds • Under the Sea • A Whole New World • Written in the Stars • You've Got a Friend in Me.
00311107 Easy Piano $14.95

CHRISTMAS FAVORITES – VOLUME 12
Blue Christmas • Frosty the Snow Man • Here Comes Santa Claus • I'll Be Home for Christmas • Silver Bells • Wonderful Christmastime • and more.
00311257 Easy Piano $14.95

CHILDREN'S SONGS – VOLUME 13
Any Dream Will Do • Do-Re-Mi • It's a Small World • Linus and Lucy • The Rainbow Connection • Splish Splash • This Land Is Your Land • Winnie the Pooh • Yellow Submarine • Zip-A-Dee-Doo-Dah.
00311258 Easy Piano $14.95

CHILDREN'S FAVORITES – VOLUME 14
Alphabet Song • Frere Jacques • Home on the Range • My Bonnie Lies over the Ocean • Oh! Susanna • Old MacDonald • This Old Man • Yankee Doodle • and more.
00311259 Easy Piano $14.95

DISNEY'S BEST – VOLUME 15
Beauty and the Beast • Bibbidi-Bobbidi-Boo • Chim Chim Cher-ee • Colors of the Wind • Friend Like Me • Hakuna Matata • Part of Your World • Someday • When She Loved Me • You'll Be in My Heart.
00311260 Easy Piano $14.95

LENNON & McCARTNEY HITS – VOLUME 16
Eleanor Rigby • Hey Jude • The Long and Winding Road • Love Me Do • Lucy in the Sky with Diamonds • Nowhere Man • Please Please Me • Sgt. Pepper's Lonely Hearts Club Band • Strawberry Fields Forever • Yesterday.
00311262 Easy Piano $14.95

HOLIDAY HITS – VOLUME 17
Christmas Time Is Here • Feliz Navidad • I Saw Mommy Kissing Santa Claus • Jingle-Bell Rock • The Most Wonderful Time of the Year • My Favorite Things • Santa Claus Is Comin' to Town • and more.
00311329 Easy Piano $14.95

HIGH SCHOOL MUSICAL – VOLUME 18
Bop to the Top • Breaking Free • Get'cha Head in the Game • Stick to the Status Quo • We're All in This Together • What I've Been Looking For • When There Was Me and You • and more.
00311752 Easy Piano $14.95

HIGH SCHOOL MUSICAL 2 – VOLUME 19
All for One • Everyday • Fabulous • Gotta Go My Own Way • I Don't Dance • What Time Is It • Work This Out • You Are the Music in Me.
00311753 Easy Piano $14.99

ANDREW LLOYD WEBBER – FAVORITES – VOLUME 20
Another Suitcase in Another Hall • Any Dream Will Do • As If We Never Said Goodbye • I Believe My Heart • Memory • Think of Me • Unexpected Song • Whistle down the Wind • You Must Love Me • and more.
00311775 Easy Piano $14.99

GREAT CLASSICAL MELODIES – VOLUME 21
Arioso • Ave Maria • Fur Elise • Jesu, Joy of Man's Desiring • Lullaby (Cradle Song) • Meditation • Ode to Joy • Romeo and Juliet (Love Theme) • Sicilienne • Theme from Swan Lake • and more.
00311776 Easy Piano $14.99

ANDREW LLOYD WEBBER – HITS – VOLUME 22
Don't Cry for Me Argentina • I Don't Know How to Love Him • Love Changes Everything • The Music of the Night • No Matter What • Wishing You Were Somehow Here Again • With One Look • and more.
00311785 Easy Piano $14.95

Prices, contents and availability subject to change without notice.

FOR MORE INFORMATION, SEE YOUR LOCAL MUSIC DEALER, OR WRITE TO:

HAL•LEONARD® CORPORATION
7777 W. BLUEMOUND RD. P.O. BOX 13819 MILWAUKEE, WI 53213

www.halleonard.com

0109

The Greatest Songs Ever Written

The Best Ever Collection
Arranged for Easy Piano with Lyrics.

The Best Broadway Songs Ever

66 songs: All I Ask of You • Cabaret • Comedy Tonight • Don't Cry for Me Argentina • Getting to Know You • If I Were a Rich Man • Memory • Ol' Man River • People • Younger Than Springtime • and many more!
00300178 ....$19.95

The Best Children's Songs Ever

102 songs: Alphabet Song • The Ballad of Davy Crockett • Bingo • A Dream Is a Wish Your Heart Makes • Eensy Weensy Spider • The Farmer in the Dell • Frere Jacques • Hello Mudduh, Hello Fadduh! • I'm Popeye the Sailor Man • Jesus Loves Me • The Muffin Man • On Top of Spaghetti • Puff the Magic Dragon • A Spoonful of Sugar • Twinkle, Twinkle Little Star • Winnie the Pooh • and more.
00310360 ....$19.95

The Best Christmas Songs Ever

69 of the most-loved songs of the season: Auld Lang Syne • Blue Christmas • The Christmas Song (Chestnuts Roasting on an Open Fire) • Feliz Navidad • Grandma Got Run Over by a Reindeer • Happy Xmas (War Is Over) • I'll Be Home for Christmas • Jingle-Bell Rock • Let It Snow! Let It Snow! Let It Snow! • My Favorite Things • Old Toy Trains • Rudolph, The Red-Nosed Reindeer • Santa Claus is Comin' to Town • Toyland • You're All I Want for Christmas • and more.
00364130 ....$18.95

The Best Contemporary Christian Songs Ever

50 songs: Awesome God • The Basics of Life • Can't Live a Day • Ed Shaddai • Father's Eyes • Great Is the Lord • His Strength Is Perfect • I Can Only Imagine • Jesus Will Still Be There • Lamb of God • Oh Lord, You're Beautiful • Place in This World • Steady On • This Is Your Time • Via Dolorosa • We Can Make a Difference • and more.
00311069 ....$18.95

The Best Country Songs Ever

78 songs, featuring: Always on My Mind • Could I Have This Dance • Crazy • Daddy Sang Bass • Forever and Ever, Amen • God Bless the U.S.A. • I Fall to Pieces • Jambalaya • King of the Road • Love Without End, Amen • Mammas, Don't Let Your Babies Grow Up to Be Cowboys • Paper Roses • Rocky Top • Sixteen Tons • Through the Years • Your Cheatin' Heart • and more.
00311540 ....$17.95

The Best Easy Listening Songs Ever

75 songs: And I Love You So • Blue Velvet • Candle on the Water • Do You Know the Way to San Jose • Don't Cry Out Loud • Feelings • The Girl from Ipanema • Hey Jude • I Write the Songs • Just Once • Love Takes Time • Make the World Go Away • Nadia's Theme • One Voice • The Rainbow Connection • Sailing • Through the Years • Unchained Melody • Vincent (Starry Starry Night) • We've Only Just Begun • You Are So Beautiful • and more.
00311119 ....$17.95

The Best Gospel Songs Ever

74 gospel songs, including: Amazing Grace • Blessed Assurance • Do Lord • Give Me That Old Time Religion • How Great Thou Art • I'll Fly Away • Just a Closer Walk with Thee • More Than Wonderful • The Old Rugged Cross • Precious Lord, Take My Hand (Take My Hand, Precious Lord) • Turn Your Radio On • The Unclouded Day • When the Roll Is Called up Yonder • Will the Circle Be Unbroken • and many more.
00310781 ....$19.95

The Best Hymns Ever

116 hymns: Amazing Grace • Beneath the Cross of Jesus • Christ the Lord Is Risen Today • Down by the Riverside • For the Beauty of the Earth • Holy, Holy, Holy • It Is Well with My Soul • Joyful, Joyful We Adore Thee • Let Us Break Bread Together • A Mighty Fortress Is Our God • The Old Rugged Cross • Rock of Ages • Were You There? • and more.
00311120 ....$17.95

The Best Jazz Standards Ever

71 jazzy tunes: Ain't Misbehavin' • Bye Bye Blackbird • Don't Get Around Much Anymore • Easy to Love • The Girl from Ipanema • It Don't Mean a Thing (If It Ain't Got That Swing) • The Lady Is a Tramp • My Funny Valentine • The Nearness of You • Old Devil Moon • Satin Doll • Stardust • Tangerine • and more.
00311091 ....$17.95

The Best Love Songs Ever

65 favorite love songs: Always • Beautiful in My Eyes • Can You Feel the Love Tonight • Endless Love • Feelings • Have I Told You Lately • Isn't It Romantic? • Just the Way You Are • Longer • My Funny Valentine • Saving All My Love for You • Vision of Love • When I Fall in Love • Your Song • and more.
00310128 ....$17.95

The Best Movie Songs Ever

71 songs: Alfie • Beauty and the Beast • Born Free • Circle of Life • Endless Love • Theme from *Jaws* • Moon River • Somewhere Out There • Speak Softly, Love • Take My Breath Away • Unchained Melody • A Whole New World • and more.
00310141...$19.95

The Best Praise & Worship Songs Ever

74 songs: Agnus Dei • Better Is One Day • Come, Now Is the Time to Worship • Days of Elijah • Firm Foundation • God of Wonders • Here I Am to Worship • I Can Only Imagine • Jesus, Lover of My Soul • Lamb of God • More Precious Than Silver • Open the Eyes of My Heart • Shine, Jesus, Shine • There Is a Redeemer • We Bow Down • You Are My King (Amazing Love) • and more.
00311312...$17.95

The Best Rock Songs Ever

More than 60 favorites: All Shook Up • Born to Be Wild • California Dreamin' • Duke of Earl • Free Bird • Great Balls of Fire • Hey Jude • I Love Rock 'N Roll • Imagine • Let It Be • My Generation • Na Na Hey Hey Kiss Him Goodbye • Oh, Pretty Woman • Rock Around the Clock • Spinning Wheel • Takin' Care of Business • Under the Boardwalk • Wild Thing • and more.
00310444...$17.95

The Best Songs Ever

71 must-own classics: All I Ask of You • Blue Skies • Call Me Irresponsible • Crazy • Edelweiss • Georgia on My Mind • Imagine • Love Me Tender • Moonlight in Vermont • My Funny Valentine • Piano Man • Satin Doll • Tears in Heaven • Unforgettable • The Way We Were • When I Fall in Love • and more.
00359223 ....$19.95

More of the Best Songs Ever

72 more classic songs: Alfie • Beyond the Sea • Come Rain or Come Shine • Don't Know Why • Every Breath You Take • The Glory of Love • Heart and Soul • In the Mood • Michelle • My Cherie Amour • The Nearness of You • One • Respect • Stand By Me • Take the "A" Train • Up Where We Belong • What'll I Do? • Young at Heart • and more.
00311090 ....$19.95

HAL LEONARD:
Your Source for the Best of Broadway

THE BEST BROADWAY SONGS EVER

Over 70 songs from Broadway's latest and greatest hit shows: As Long as He Needs Me • Bess, You Is My Woman • Bewitched • Comedy Tonight • Don't Cry for Me Argentina • Getting to Know You • I Could Have Danced All Night • I Dreamed a Dream • If I Were a Rich Man • The Last Night of the World • Love Changes Everything • Oklahoma • Ol' Man River • People • Try to Remember • and more.
00309155 Piano/Vocal/Guitar $24.95

THE BIG BOOK OF BROADWAY

This edition includes 70 songs from classic musicals and recent blockbusters like *The Producers, Aida* and *Hairspray*. Includes: Bring Him Home • Camelot • Everything's Coming Up Roses • The Impossible Dream • A Lot of Livin' to Do • One • Some Enchanted Evening • Thoroughly Modern Millie • Till There Was You • and more.
00311658 Piano/Vocal/Guitar $19.95

BROADWAY CLASSICS
PIANO PLAY-ALONG SERIES, VOLUME 4

This book/CD pack provides keyboardists with a full performance track and a separate backing track for each tune. Songs include: Ain't Misbehavin' • Cabaret • If I Were a Bell • Memory • Oklahoma • Some Enchanted Evening • The Sound of Music • You'll Never Walk Alone.
00311075 Book/CD Pack $14.95

BROADWAY DELUXE

125 of Broadway's biggest show tunes! Includes such showstoppers as: Bewitched • Cabaret • Camelot • Day by Day • Hello Young Lovers • I Could Have Danced All Night • I Talk to the Trees • I've Grown Accustomed to Her Face • If Ever I Would Leave You • The Lady Is a Tramp • My Heart Belongs to Daddy • Oklahoma • September Song • Seventy Six Trombones • Try to Remember • and more!
00309245 Piano/Vocal/Guitar $24.95

BROADWAY SONGS

Get more bang for your buck with this jam-packed collection of 73 songs from 56 shows, including *Annie Get Your Gun, Cabaret, The Full Monty, Jekyll & Hyde, Les Misérables, Oklahoma* and more. Songs: Any Dream Will Do • Consider Yourself • Footloose • Getting to Know You • I Dreamed a Dream • One • People • Summer Nights • The Surrey with the Fringe on Top • With One Look • and more.
00310832 Piano/Vocal/Guitar $12.95

CONTEMPORARY BROADWAY

44 songs from 25 contemporary musicals and Broadway revivals. Includes: And All That Jazz (*Chicago*) • Dancing Queen (*Mamma Mia!*) • Good Morning Baltimore (*Hairspray*) • Mein Herr (*Cabaret*) • Popular (*Wicked*) • Purpose (*Avenue Q*) • Seasons of Love (*Rent*) • When You Got It, Flaunt It (*The Producers*) • You Rule My World (*The Full Monty*) • and more.
00310796 Piano/Vocal/Guitar $18.95

DEFINITIVE BROADWAY

142 of the greatest show tunes ever, including: Don't Cry for Me Argentina • Hello, Dolly! • I Dreamed a Dream • Lullaby of Broadway • Mack the Knife • Memory • Send in the Clowns • Somewhere • The Sound of Music • Strike Up the Band • Summertime • Sunrise, Sunset • Tea for Two • Tomorrow • What I Did for Love • and more.
00359570 Piano/Vocal/Guitar $24.95

ESSENTIAL SONGS: BROADWAY

Over 100 songs are included in this top-notch collection: Any Dream Will Do • Blue Skies • Cabaret • Don't Cry for Me, Argentina • Edelweiss • Hello, Dolly! • I'll Be Seeing You • Memory • The Music of the Night • Oklahoma • Seasons of Love • Summer Nights • There's No Business like Show Business • Tomorrow • and more.
00311222 Piano/Vocal/Guitar $24.95

KIDS' BROADWAY SONGBOOK

An unprecedented collection of songs originally performed by children on the Broadway stage. Includes 16 songs for boys and girls, including: Gary, Indiana (*The Music Man*) • Castle on a Cloud (*Les Misérables*) • Where Is Love? (*Oliver!*) • Tomorrow (*Annie*) • and more.
00311609 Book Only $14.95
00740149 Book/CD Pack $24.99

THE OFF-BROADWAY SONGBOOK

42 gems from off-Broadway hits, including *Godspell, Tick Tick...Boom!, The Fantasticks, Once upon a Mattress, The Wild Party* and more. Songs include: Always a Bridesmaid • Come to Your Senses • Day by Day • Happiness • How Glory Goes • I Hate Musicals • The Picture in the Hall • Soon It's Gonna Rain • Stars and the Moon • Still Hurting • Twilight • and more.
00311168 Piano/Vocal/Guitar $16.95

THE TONY AWARDS SONGBOOK

This collection assembles songs from each of Tony-winning Best Musicals through "Mama Who Bore Me" from 2007 winner *Spring Awakening*. Songs include: Til There Was You • The Sound of Music • Hello, Dolly! • Sunrise, Sunset • Send in the Clowns • Tomorrow • Memory • I Dreamed a Dream • Seasons of Love • Circle of Life • Mama, I'm a Big Girl Now • and more. Includes photos and a table of contents listed both chronologically and alphabetically.
00311092 Piano/Vocal/Guitar $19.95

THE ULTIMATE BROADWAY FAKE BOOK

Over 700 songs from more than 200 Broadway shows! Songs include: All I Ask of You • Bewitched • Cabaret • Don't Cry for Me Argentina • Edelweiss • Getting to Know You • Hello, Dolly! • If I Were a Rich Man • Last Night of the World • The Music of the Night • Oklahoma • People • Seasons of Love • Tell Me on a Sunday • Unexpected Song • and more!
00240046 Melody/Lyrics/Chords $47.50

ULTIMATE BROADWAY PLATINUM

100 popular Broadway songs: As If We Never Said Goodbye • Bye Bye Birdie • Camelot • Everything's Coming Up Roses • Gigi • Hello, Young Lovers • I Enjoy Being a Girl • Just in Time • My Favorite Things • On a Clear Day • People • Sun and Moon • Try to Remember • Who Can I Turn To • Younger Than Springtime • and many more.
00311496 Piano/Vocal/Guitar $22.95

Prices, contents, and availability subject to change without notice.
Some products may not be available outside the U.S.A.

FOR MORE INFORMATION, SEE YOUR LOCAL MUSIC DEALER,
OR WRITE TO:

HAL•LEONARD® CORPORATION

7777 W. BLUEMOUND RD. P.O. BOX 13819 MILWAUKEE, WI 53213

Get complete songlists and more at www.halleonard.com

0209